AN E3 BOOK FROM

E³ Experts
Educating
Entrepreneurs

Co-Authored by E3 Co-Founders:

Michelle Ketterman and Alicia White

Visit E3's website etimes3.info where
entrepreneurs share real advice and proven action
steps to help you build a successful business.

Published by:

911 *i*Publishing

911 iPublishing
PO Box 845
Wylie, TX 75098
911iPublishing.com
800-313-5911 x304

TABLE OF CONTENTS

DEDICATIONS

This book is dedicated to Mr. Wonderful for encouraging me to chase my dream. Thank you for never trying to hold me back.

— Michelle

Rick, I dedicate this book to you. My success is because of you and what you have taught me over the years. Your never-ending love, support, and encouragement has blessed me in so many ways.

—Alicia

PREFACE

Do you wonder how to turn your ideas into a profitable business? Do you have a strong yearning to be your own boss? Have you spent countless hours researching to only lead to more questions?

We understand because we've been there. That's why Michelle Ketterman and Alicia White founded Experts Educating Entrepreneurs (E3), to provide information to help beginning business owners and entrepreneurs succeed in their new business. Our books will guide you in a variety of topics and provide insight into what works and what does not.

E3's first edition focuses on two topics that every budding entrepreneur needs to know about:

Get Forward Focused...N O W ! by Michelle Ketterman

Design Tips that Win Customers by Alicia White

We hope you will enjoy our first book and are eager to read more. Future projects will have topics ranging from networking, and marketing to legal matters and goal setting. E3 selects contributing authors known as the experts in their field. Be assured that the advice you read is valid and useful information and ethically sound to help you grow your business.

Now for the legal stuff:

Whether you are new to owning a business or simply need a few refreshers on operating a business, E3 will give you valuable insight to starting and owning a business.

Please note that much of this publication is based on personal experience. Although the author(s) and publisher have made every reasonable attempt to achieve complete accuracy of the content in this publication, they assume no responsibility for errors or omissions. Also, you should use this information as you see fit and at your own risk. Your particular situation may not be exactly suited to the examples illustrated here; in fact, it is likely that they will not be the same, and you should adjust your use of the information and recommendations accordingly.

Any trademarks, service marks, product names, or named features are assumed to be the property of their respective owners, and are used only for reference. There is no implied endorsement if we use one of these terms.

Finally, use your head. Nothing in this publication is intended to replace common sense, legal, medical, or other professional advice, and is meant to inform and entertain the reader.

LET THE LEARNING BEGIN!

WHO IS E3?

Michelle Ketterman, E3 Co-Founder; Owner of The Inventory Experts; Founder of The Inventory Institute; Published Author

Violated first by a home robbery and then by her inability to file an accurate insurance claim, Michelle Ketterman founded The Inventory Experts. The Inventory Experts compiles comprehensive third-party reports that document items in homes and businesses including serial and model numbers and detailed photographs.

After years in the profession, Michelle made a few shocking discoveries: 1) over half of the professionals claimed to be licensed although none existed in any state; 2) with no industry oversight or accountability, most industry products were not completely forthright about accolades, testimonials, or credentials; 3) over 45% of current Inventory professionals closed their doors each year.

These discoveries led Michelle to form The Inventory Institute in 2009; a national initiative where North American Inventory Professionals and related products can collaborate, learn, and be unbiasedly credentialed. Consumers can also learn how to self-compile their inventory, the benefits of hiring a third-party Inventory Professional, and find pre-screened professionals. Michelle single handedly created the nation's first Home Inventory Professional Certification program, Code of Conduct, and Professional Code of Standards.

Michelle has since added a Home Inventory Mastery Program, HIP Coaching, HIP Coaching Academy, various training Inventory products and services, and allows experienced executives to join The Inventory Experts' family by operating an independent office of The Inventory Experts in their town. Michelle teaches professionals how to launch a Home Inventory career, become certified, and learn how to increase their businesses profitability, or become industry leaders and HIP coaches. Michelle is known nationally as "The Inventory Expert."

A co-founder of E3, Michelle is passionate about helping entrepreneurs avoid the pitfalls and expensive shenanigans often encountered by new business owners. She focuses a lot of energy assisting entrepreneurs navigate through the many advertising, time management, organization, set-up, and day to day operational options available.

Michelle has written over 15 inventory profession books, including *The Home Inventory Profession...How to be an Expert* which was nominated for a 2012 Small Business Book award.

Michelle is an active Toastmaster and networker. She is president of several networking chapters and regularly facilitates high-level master mind, brainstorming, and roadmapping sessions. She has been named Top 10 Networker in Dallas by *Be the Boss Magazine* and The 2011 #47 Networker in America by Perfect Networker.

For more information, please visit one of Michelle's websites:
More About Michelle: MichelleKetterman.com
The Inventory Experts: ProveItsYours.com
The Inventory Institute: TheInventoryInstitute.com

Alicia White, E3 Co-Founder; Owner of Back of the Room Productions and 911 iDesigns; Co-Owner of Incident Page; Published Photographer

Alicia White, author and founder of Back of the Room Productions, creates compelling products for speakers, authors, coaches, and presenters whose public image demands high quality professional brand presentation. She is the first in the nation to provide customized packaging to speakers for their back of the room sales and marketing.

Clients from many different industries benefit from Alicia's vast experience in print media, graphic design, photography, and content creation. She leverages these creative processes to help guide the design of her client's projects. With the goal of consistency always in mind, high quality brand imagery across all marketing pieces helps her clients attract customers willing to pay top dollar.

Through experiences as the founder of two businesses and co-owner of a nationally recognized company, Alicia has gained considerable knowledge pertaining to operating a successful business. Her enthusiasm for detail and organization and keen ability to build lasting, positive relationships allows her to help others realize their business goals. Alicia's leadership experience in non-profit organizations, local politics and community, and mastermind groups are a benefit to anyone seeking advice on how to run a business and garner lasting relationships.

Although she is a "sweet southern girl," Alicia is also a respected business woman with a savvy understanding of how to live life to its fullest. Alicia and her husband Rick travel to United States National Parks to photograph riveting wildlife and stunning landscapes. Alicia serves as a volunteer for a Texas-based fire department photographing the raw bravery of firefighters. A few of her firefighting photos are forever immortalized in Wylie, Texas' first commissioned mural art piece. Her photos are a local art gallery favorite.

To learn more about the services Alicia provides, please visit:
Products for Speakers: BackoftheRoomProductions.com
Design and Print: 911iDesigns.com
Book and Calendar Publishing: 911iPublishing.com

GET FORWARD FOCUSED...N O W !

by Michelle Ketterman, E3 Co-Founder

The key is in not spending time, but in investing it. — Stephen R. Covey

Imagine how much more prepared you would be today if you had the ability to get a bird's eye view of last week, last month, or even last year. You can and it is easier than you can imagine. It is incredibly simple and easy to implement and can prove to be invaluable to any business owner.

Did you ever sit down with the absolute best intentions of compiling a To Do List and then become so overwhelmed or distracted you never finished it? Recognized experts agree that successful entrepreneurs regularly use To Do Lists, take thorough notes, and are generally organized and very focused. Like many of us, I own and operate more than one business; I own three businesses, run a national organization, and train new professionals in my industry and regularly attend networking events around the country.

With just a few strategic minutes every day and the right tools and processes in place, you will be amazed how productive and efficient YOU too can be.

First Things First

Before becoming a super-human productivity machine, a few steps are necessary. Take a really good look at your business plan, mission statement, and the general vision of your business and recommit to your goals and purpose. Make sure you are still as dedicated to your business as you should be. You MUST be in love with your business or you will never find the time or motivation needed to be as successful and profitable as possible. If you doubt your level of a'mour for your business, asking these questions might help you honestly reevaluate your passion and commitment to your business:

- Do I still eagerly look forward to work everyday?
- Are there exciting projects in my pipeline?
- Is my business thriving financially and productively?
- Do I have a clear vision for the next year, 5 years, 10 years, etc?
- Am I living my passion?
- Does work recharge my battery and give me a solid sense of accomplishment and pride?

So You ARE Still in Love...

Your business has passed the review and litmus love test — congratulations! Now you are ready to roll up your sleeves and focus...really focus. Get ready for major leaps forward!

No More To Do Lists!

Before beginning your renewed business focus with clarity, you must remove the term "To Do List" from your vocabulary. Historically, To Dos wear us down, muddle our days, and become a nuisance and chore. Daily To Do Lists are easy to "forget" now and then and even easier to stop doing all together. Instead of a To Do List, create a Forward Focus Log that spells out your day; every aspect of your well-rounded day.

As entrepreneurs, on any given day we work on much more than just our business. We have homes, families, hobbies, volunteering, errands, and countless other things. Do not make the same mistake so many people do when they have one planner for work and a separate planner for personal things. Your Forward Focus Log should include everything you need and plan to address on any given day. Success happens much faster and easier when you are able to see and arrange your entire day in one place. So let's get started!

Put Your Entire Day on Paper

I use an on-line calendar AND a paper calendar. As "plugged in" as I try to be, the reality of my work is that I often meet with clients and schedule follow-up meetings without access to my on-line calendar. Because of this, I must maintain both a paper and an on-line calendar and I find it easiest to keep my Daily Forward Focus Log in the same binder as my monthly planner.

What to Have on Your Daily Forward Focus Log

Although there are many topics to consider adding to your Daily Forward Focus Log, sticking to the core topics will probably work best (at least when you first begin using a Daily Forward Focus Log). Consider what topics you have on your business plan and goals.

I recommend starting with these topics:

- **Spirituality**

  - Set your **daily intention.** Use this section to define your daily intention. It is VITALLY important to set your daily intention and then put it to paper. This may seem a bit odd to some, but it can literally make the difference between mediocre success and skyrocketing to the finish line sooner than imagined.

  - Write the **quote of the day.** When this section is added to a Daily Forward Focus Log, your mind pays more attention to the quotes posted daily on various social media sites. Quite often, the absolute perfect quote for your circumstance on any given day will appear. By using this section when the perfect quote appears, you will have somewhere to keep the quote, and the quote will remain in your attention for the entire day and can be referred to later.

  - **Prayer & Meditation.** Not only is this a great place to log your prayer or meditation time for the day, it is also the perfect way to keep track of your daily devotional time.

  - Other possible topics for this section include Church, bible study, chanting, group fellowship, and so on.

- **Physical**

  - The best place to log your **workouts.** If you do not typically work out, use it to keep track of extra steps or the 10 minute walk around the block, or every time you take the stairs instead of the elevator. This section is a great place to remind you to take regular breaks.

○ **Self-care** is one of the most important things entrepreneurs can do. In today's world where everyone constantly is plugged in and turned on, we all need to take extra measures to take care of ourselves in what makes the most sense to each of us. Did you get a massage or a manicure? Maybe you took a long bath, had a professional shave, got your shoes shined, or went for a hike. Regardless of what you did to pamper yourself, log it. If you are not doing one self-care activity every day, start TODAY!

○ Other possible topics for this section include hobby time, quiet time, afternoon power-nap, and so on.

● **Business**

○ **Social Media.** I know, I've heard it 1000 times before, "I just don't have time for social media." The world has changed and if you have time to answer your phone, you have time for social media! The days of sending postcards and cold calling are over. The consumer of today wants to find you; and they want to find you by researching you, your business, and your reputation. The best (and coincidentally least expensive) way to spread the word about your business is through social media. Period. Bottom line. To be successful in today's marketplace and remain competitive, social media is a must. It is way too easy to forget about daily social media. On the other hand, it is also way too easy to get lost on social media sites. To make sure you meet your social media goals without losing yourself on the various sites, include social media on your Daily Forward Focus Log.

○ **Blog/Articles/Writing.** Using the same principles as social media above, use this section to log and maintain your blog and other writing goals.

○ **Networking/Mixers.** The old adage "it's not what you know, but who you know" still holds true. Even in today's on-line community, as important as remaining a positive on-line presence is, entrepreneurs still need to get out there and network, network, network. Use this section to monitor meetings and mixers. This is the perfect place to keep track of how many business cards collected, one-on-ones scheduled, or possible referral partners met.

○ **Reaching Out.** Statistics show that entrepreneurs do not connect with existing clients and strategic partners to generate more business. Keeping this section on the Daily Forward Focus Log ensures that you never lose sight of the fact that reaching out via personal phone calls, emails, and USPS cards is relevant. Maintaining these crucial relationships must continue to stay high on every entrepreneur's Daily Forward Focus Log; this section ensures that it does.

○ **Miscellaneous.** Other possible topics for this section include speaking opportunities, radio show appearances, one-on-ones, news coverage, and so on.

- **To Do**

    - ○ **Done.** A place to indicate the task has been completed.

    - ○ **Priority.** Once all of your daily tasks are listed, they need to be prioritized for obvious reasons.

    - ○ **Task.** Write down at least 10 things you need to get done today. (More on this later.)

- **Tomorrow I will focus on**

    - ○ Self explanatory, this is typically one sentence written at the end of the work day. (More on this later.)

What to NOT Have on Your Daily Forward Focus Log

A Daily Forward Focus Log has many roles and helps with several areas of an entrepreneur's life. Remember that your Daily Forward Focus Log should represent a bird's eye view of what you envision and plan for the day. It is often reviewed days, weeks, or even months after it was initially used and should serve as a high level summary of your day. However, many things do NOT belong on a Daily Forward Focus Log including:

- **Grocery or office supply list.** While "pick up groceries" or "run to Office Depot" may very well be on your Log, the entire shopping list does not belong on this page. I keep my grocery and office supply lists current with Evernote.com. This program allows me to keep any list I want on my computer

(Mac or PC) and syncs my lists to my account on my iPhone. Talk about convenient... I simply could not live without Evernote.

- **Message Log.** Tracking voice and email messages on your Daily Forward Focus Log takes up a lot of space and muddles the 'bird's eye' view of your day. They should be tracked elsewhere.

- **Accounts Payable and Receivables.** Although process invoices, deposit checks, or send customer receipts should be on a Daily Forward Focus Log, tracking specific invoices, payments, and correspondence needs to be tracked and logged elsewhere.

- **Mileage Counter.** Do not track mileage on a Daily Forward Focus Log. Mileage counters are typically stored in a vehicle. If your Daily Forward Focus Log is stored in your vehicle, you are doing something drastically wrong because it should be within arm's reach all day long.

How to Work on Your Daily Forward Focus Log

Contrary to what many of us were taught, writing pages and pages of countless To Dos is NOT the most productive thing entrepreneurs can do. Ironically, the exercise of creating list after list is counterproductive. To stay focused and accomplish as much as possible, entrepreneurs need to have short, digestible, and concentrated assignments. Think of it this way: as a busy entrepreneur, how likely are you to work your way through six pages of lists with 50-100 tasks?

Realistically, not very likely at all; in fact, you are more likely to throw your hands up in defeat. On the other hand, an entire day of tasks and priorities laid out on one page in front of you makes it difficult to NOT have a successful day.

Subconsciously, when faced with an enormous list of endless tasks, the majority of us will either run for the hills or find anything (I mean anything) else to do; anything other than work our way through this enormous and intimidating list. To avoid setting yourself up for failure, NEVER create a Daily Forward Focus Log more than one page long. If you are especially productive and complete your entire Daily Forward Focus Log, it's perfectly OK to fill out an additional log for the same day. However, do NOT start a new Daily Forward Focus Log unless the current page is 100% completed — no exceptions including every section. Otherwise, you will end up with a lot of half completed Daily Forward Focus Logs.

When Compiling your Forward Focus Log

- Think about what you plan to accomplish, current on-going projects and tasks along with future projects.

- Only have 7 to 10 extra logs pre-printed. This give you the ability to add items and categories without wasting paper and resources. As silly as it may seem, this holds some people back, so eliminate that worry and only keep a few copies on hand.

- Keep them together in one place. Every Monday, I remove the previous week's Daily Forward Focus Logs and place them in a file folder dedicated to old logs. At the end of every quarter, I scan the Daily

Forward Focus Logs from previous quarter and upload them to my on-line file folder. I do not throw the paper copies away until one year after their original date. For example, I keep second quarter 2010 Daily Forward Focus Logs until the end of the second quarter in 2011; this way I always have the 12 most previous historical months for easy access and review.

- My printed calendar is on 11″ x 17″ paper that is folded in half and kept in a binder. My Daily Forward Focus Logs for the week are kept in the fold. At times, I will use the back of the previous Daily Forward Focus Log to take notes or jot down important items and details.

- Do not begin the next Daily Forward Focus Log until that morning. In other words, do not start your next day log the night before. Always start the day of. This should not be an on-going multi-page document, but a document started with a fresh piece of paper and a fresh perspective every morning.

On the next page is a generic Daily Forward Focus Log to begin formatting yours. Choose words and actions that best fit your needs and say good-bye to those To Do Lists!

Remember your Daily Forward Focus Log is a productivity tool. Always keep an open mind and look for ways to improve and expand your Daily Forward Focus Log. If you are skeptical, try a Daily Forward Focus Log for two weeks and your will be stunned at your increase in productivity!

SPIRITUALITY:

My intentions for today are:

Today's quote:

MEDITATION/PRAYER: *What:*   *Time:*   *Other:*

PHYSICAL:

WORK OUT: *Time:*   *Distance:*   *Other:*

SELF-CARE: *(massage, Yoga, manicure)*

MISC:

BUSINESS:

TWITTER: **FACEBOOK:**   *Other:*

BLOG/ARTICLE/WRITING:

NETWORKING/MIXER:

REACHING OUT:

MISC:

TODAY'S TO DO:

Done	Priority	Task	Done	Priority	Task

Tomorrow I will focus on:

DESIGN TIPS THAT WIN CUSTOMERS

By Alicia White, E3 Co-Founder

When creating a marketing piece to promote your business, it should not come as a surprise that your customers will respect you as a business if your marketing materials are presented in a professional and appealing manner.

This can include the type of paper you use to print on, the type of font selected to present your message, to color choices. Messages can be printed in a corporate, matter of fact style or by using a sense of humor or perhaps whimsical approach. Choosing the method in which to present your message depends on a few factors. If your product or service is highly creative, adding whimsy to your message is a great way to attract the kind of customers you want. If your services are more serious in nature, create your message so that it is to the point, providing factual information.

TIP: Using humor is a great way to approach heavy-handed or not-so-pleasant subjects. For example, I met a plumber whose tag line is "Your number two business is our number one business." If you decide to add some levity to a subject, be sure your target audience will understand your sense of humor. There is nothing worse than offending an existing or potential client because of poor humor or telling an inside joke that they may not understand. To avoid this, create a focus group of people who don't really know you (maybe some people you've began networking with). Ask them to partake in your study and see what the results are. If the results are positive — go for it! If not — don't give up and try again. People remember those who make them laugh or smile.

Regardless of how you choose to share your message, there are several factors you must consider when creating your marketing materials. In Part One, you will learn the importance of the three Cs that are used in every marketing campaign. In Part Two, you will gain insight into how the experts create and print quality, professional marketing materials.

The Three Cs

If you ask any design, copy writing, or marketing expert, they will tell you that there are three "Cs" to every marketing campaign. They are:

Creative

Consistent

Concise

Each of the three Cs work to help build a solid, professional business image and create effective marketing while maintaining strong identity branding.

Creative

It is hard for someone who is not naturally artistic to produce something visually creative. However, creativity does not necessarily have to be in the visual sense; it can apply to be in how something functions. Take for example the toothbrush. Not a work of art, mind you, but it is creative in function. Imagine what people used to use in the old days to clean their teeth: sticks, twigs, feathers, and quills! Today technology has created a way to hold tiny bristles on the head of a toothbrush to clean teeth. A creative development for better function!

Being creative means producing a piece that captures your audience's attention. This can be done by developing a unique logo, designing a printed piece that visually appeals to your target audience, or presenting your message in a clever way. For example, you do not have to conform to the standard 8.5" x 11" sell sheet/flyer or the 4" x 6" postcard. There are many ways to make your marketing collateral creative and stand out from the competition.

One marketing campaign I worked on involved placing technical information onto a poster. Typically, this information was mailed to clients as an 8.5" x 11" eight-page publication on white paper stapled at the top. Nothing wrong with that method but it wasn't fancy either.

Fortunately, we had some insight about this project. We learned from our customers that they referred to the publication almost daily. After some brainstorming, I designed a colorful poster, clearly providing all of the information in an easy to use format. Customers loved the piece and proudly displayed the poster on their office walls.

Creative yet functional design

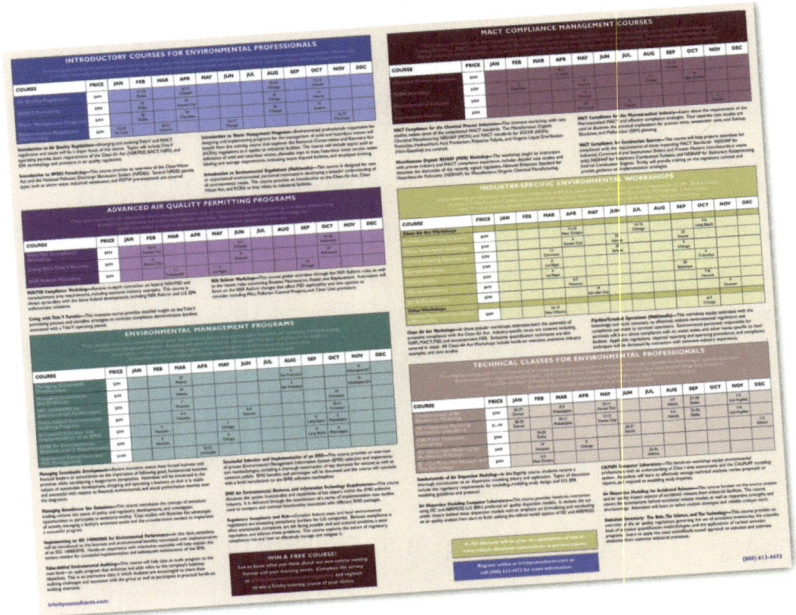

As for being visually creative, some people have it and some don't. Some people are easily inspired by works of art, nature, or architecture and others simply can't "see it" and leave design to the professionals. I'm not talking about not being able to draw a straight line or paint a pretty picture. If my livelihood relied on that, I'd be broke! I'm talking about how creative people can mesh the right colors in the right spot to make the perfect visual or use interesting type treatment. Creativity can be as bold as one of Andy Warhol's paintings or as simple as McDonald's golden arches.

Beauty really is in the eye of the beholder and you, as a business owner, must determine the direction your business image will take. Just because you aren't using flowing swirls or colorful circles or ink splatters in your design doesn't mean you aren't creative. Ask yourself these questions when you design marketing collateral:

- Are your materials visually captivating?
- Are images used to present your product or service accurately and effectively?
- Are the colors inviting and true to your industry?

Take note of other factors; word placement, typography choices, and copy writing all play a part in creativity.

TIP: As mentioned earlier, creativity comes in all forms especially when working with a small budget. One client came to me with an idea but had absolutely no budget. She wanted a 9" x 12" folder with four 8.5" x 11" sell sheets. She didn't need many (only 100) because she was marketing to a warm prospect list. After informing her of the cost for such a project, we had to get creative — she had no budget! So I designed an economical postcard with a web address that directed her prospects to a full blown electronic media kit. I designed the sell sheets, just as I would for print, and saved the files as an Adobe Acrobat PDF file that were placed on her web site. She also offered her prospects the media kit via e-mail.

Consistent

In today's market, one thing is for sure, to achieve success you must be consistent. This applies to most processes. One such process is to place your logo on your marketing materials in the same place each and every time. Include any appropriate contact info along with your logo such as a web site or phone number, but always place your logo and that info in the same spot each and every time. Once a person sees your advertising materials repeatedly, they will recall your business image and it will be easily recollected when it comes time for them to make a purchase decision.

Advertising is another area in which consistency is needed. If you are purchasing advertising in a publication, it is important to create your ad so that your logo and contact info is placed in the same spot each time. You also want to consider placing the ad in the same page location each time you advertise. Here's a tip: Because of how people flip through a book or magazine, the right side gets most views. Sounds odd but try it out for yourself. Grab a magazine and look at the cover. With your thumb resting on right side, flip through the pages. Where does your eye land? On the right side. Some publications charge a little more for that space because they recognize its importance.

Advertising is not for print only. TV commercials, Internet radio, viral videos, and even networking events are great opportunities to market your business. Being consistent in the look and feel of your business image and product or services will help build your branding identity one visual, one sound, one touch at a time. Think of your favorite song that you sing out loud. Did you look up the lyrics? You probably learned the lyrics like most people do. By listening to it over and over again. Build your brand through repetition.

Repetition builds your reputation!

And that brings us to this: **the need for consistency also lies heavily in how often you promote your message**. Are you placing your ads in a publication once a year? Unless your target audience only picks up this publication once every year, stop. You are not branding effectively. Try an ad campaign.

This involves finding a publication directed to your target audience. If you sell jewelry, you are less likely to find customers in a home building magazine rather than a fashion magazine. Try placing a minimum of four ads; six is better; and if you have the budget, twelve is best. Take note of the publication's frequency: daily, weekly, monthly, quarterly. As phone calls come in, ask how they heard about your company and then evaluate the answers. If the results are not what you expected then perhaps change the frequency or try a new look. You can do this for any kind of campaign such as the Internet, e-mail, direct mail, or radio promotions.

How about a postcard campaign? Perfect, if you do it correctly. Sending only one postcard will not effectively build your brand. People need to see your identity over and over again before it catches on. Try mailing multiple postcards over a period of time. Keep the postcards consistent in look and have a similar message. Offer something — anything — whether it's a free trial or discount and then evaluate your results. Remember, the more consistent you are in repetitive acts, the more likely people are going to remember you.

TIP: Do you network? If so, try starting or ending your elevator speech the same way each and every time. For example, start by peaking your name, company name, and company motto; over time people will remember you and your message. This is where "consistency" plays a major role. Also, the more unique you are in your message the better your business image carries.

Concise

Concise. Succinct. Brief. Short. Direct.

The above string of words could easily serve as the end of this portion of this section but it goes a little deeper than that. Often times, businesses say more in their advertising than is really needed. I have seen this happen from the beginning of my career in each and every industry, and not once have I been challenged to work with just three words. Clients have asked me to design a postcard around a two page document or create a standard tri-fold brochure with over 6,000 words. Unless you are writing a book or building an in depth web site, there is no need for this many words.

Your customers are just as busy as you are. If the goal is to create a marketing piece that will grab customer attention at a quick glance, you cannot assault them with a bucket load of words hoping they will actually put down the rest of their mail pile and read every word written. It will not happen.

TIP: Does your company name say exactly what you do? If not and your company is not nationally known, consider developing a tag line or company motto. For example, if someone tells me their company name is Rettop, that doesn't tell me anything. Let's say this is a tap dancing company. We could supplement with a tag line that is more specific like "Put a little tap in your life." Ah, okay. "Rettop — Put a little tap in your life!" Adding a tag line nicely sums up this business.

Write Tight. This phrase was embedded in me in college when I was learning to write for newspapers. There is only so much space in a newspaper column so we were forced to cut our articles in half. The editor then removed one third of the last round of revisions to make the article fit. **Say less, mean more.** Use these tips to write tight:

- Use words that succinctly describe what you want to get across.
- Use bullet points.
- Pick three or four words and use spacers such as dashes and periods to separate them. For example: "Quality. Service. Compassion."
- Use key words in phrases to get your point across.

I once designed a billboard for a client; actually I designed two and I'll explain why. The client wanted to place a statement at the very top of the billboard along with logo contact number, slogan, established date, a photo, and so on, and so on. I advised strongly against placing that much information on the billboard. She declined, which was her right. I then asked her to consider removing the long twelve word statement she wanted at the top of the billboard. She again declined.

The billboard was beautiful. The photo was great, the logo and contact info clearly seen, even the sentence was visible from the road — but not at 60 mph. I drove by the billboard and all I saw was the photo and the logo. A week later I was re-hired to design a new, more concise billboard to replace the beautiful, not-so-concise billboard.

Beautiful billboard but the message was missed at 60 mph

First Bank doesn't just assist the communities we serve,
we help build them.

FIRST BANK
Est. 1885

www.firstbankfarmersville.com
Community. Success. First Bank.

Farmersville | 223 McKinney Street | 972.782.6181

Member **FDIC**

Sometimes a few words and a pop of color is all that is needed

First Then. First Now.

FIRST BANK

Est. 1885

Member **FDIC**

FARMERSVILLE · LAVON · PRINCETON
firstbankfarmersville.com

The moral to the story is: think of how your publication will be viewed. Will your audience receive your literature in the mail as a promotion for your services? Or are you developing a media kit where an abundance of information is required? Or will your clients be driving past at 60 mph? Determine the function first and design from there.

Part Two: How the Experts Make You Look Good

When presenting your business image, you of course want your marketing collateral to look professional and be a high quality show piece. Your marketing collateral is a reflection of you and your company. Whatever piece you leave behind must present the image and message you are trying to share. You may have Zig Ziglar's motivational sales skills but if your marketing literature does not support this, then are you really giving the best impression?

Let's say you meet with a potential client. Your presentation bowled him over. He is ready to sign up today. But he is not the decision maker. He has to go to his boss and tell him about you and your services. Bluntly put, he has to sell you to his boss. If you have left behind a presentation that isn't professional or doesn't represent the quality that your business image is built upon, his boss is going to look elsewhere because there are several more companies out there who do what you do. And many of those companies ensure their marketing materials are top notch. You need top notch marketing literature, too!

Even non-profit organizations can enjoy stylish design!

So what does this mean? It means hiring a professional designer and having your marketing materials printed professionally. I know, I know. You don't have the budget — right now. And that's okay, you have to start somewhere. Instead of printing your business cards on your printer at home, use a free business card printing service. If you are still doing this after a month or two, you need to really determine if you are serious about your business or not. It is okay to tell folks your cards are temporary until you get them professionally designed, but if they see you handing out the same cards with a generic design template after a couple of months, people won't take you as seriously as you would like. Everyone knows what the "free" cards look like. Don't leave that impression.

What does it take to have your information printed professionally? Most designers have a list of dos and don'ts. Mine are simply: if you don't have the information, I can't create it. I've created a basic list of items I need to create a professional marketing piece. Keep reading to learn why these items are important in building your business image.

The right sized images for a project: Use photos professionally made or learn how to take high resolution photographs. Understand the limitations. **Important: web images CAN NOT be used for printed materials.** Do not ask your designer to "just pull the images off of the web site." Even more important: if you do not have images, do not ask your designer to copy photos from the Internet. This is illegal! Purchase stock photographs from reputable stock photography sites. There are dozens with high resolution images for a low price.

Your company logo in vector format: I can't stress this enough: there is a difference between an image that has been created with a vector program like Illustrator and an image created in a raster program like Photoshop. There ARE limitations to raster logos. You cannot scale files larger than the original size and expect good results. You may think your logo is a vector because it can be opened in a vector program. This is not always true. Raster images can be placed along with vector images in a vector file. If you provide a logo containing raster images, most likely it will need to be converted to a true native vector file. The investment will be worth it in the long run. Note: if you have had business cards printed or a promotional product printed, ask your vendor if they have your logo in vector format.

Copy (the words used in your message): What is the message you want to share? Are you offering something? Announcing a new product or service? Often times clients will provide a Word document with everything they want to say. That is wonderful! Just be sure you know that depending on the project, some of the copy may have to be cut. If you do not intend to write the language, ask your designer if they can do that for you or find a copywriter who will learn about your business and sell your product or services through copy.

Direction from you: What style do you want this piece to be? Where do you see your logo and tag line going? How do you visualize the final copy? What is the most important thing you want to get across to your target audience? I've helped customers who have had absolutely no idea what they want. When faced with this, I ask them to send links to web sites, PDFs, or e-brochures to give me an idea of what they are looking for. This guides me in the creative process; nine times out of ten, I can hit the mark on the first concept. If you are unsure how you want your literature to look, send ideas that appeal to you to your designer.

Budget: Yes, we need to know your budget. This is not a ploy to see how much we can "make off of you." This helps us gauge how to proceed in the bidding process. We don't want to bid on an idea that may be out of reach. We genuinely want to help you and if we have an idea of your budget no matter how big or small, we will come up with creative ways to promote your business; even if it means printing ten versus 1,000. If you have a healthy budget, then let us know so we can present stellar printing techniques such as Spot UV, special folds, or die cuts to help your marketing literature stand out from the competition.

Time: Creative design, professional printing, and maintaining a budget takes times. If you want it fast, be prepared to pay rush fees. Give yourself enough time:

- to think about what you wish to achieve;
- for the designer to implement your idea; and
- for the piece to be printed and delivered.

One month is usually enough time for a professionally developed brochure, annual report, or newsletter. Other marketing pieces can be developed quicker such as banners or business cards. Whereas marketing campaigns, in which several pieces are developed and delivered, will take much longer. However, the time required boils down to you. Yes, YOU need to get the information to the designer in a timely manner. If you need a brochure printed and delivered in six weeks, do not wait until week four to supply the information needed to the designer. If you wait, expect to pay rush fees.

In a Nutshell

We all know that looking your best is imperative when building business; that starts with a solid understanding of good design. These tips should help you achieve professional design. If you have the creativity and the skills to produce an industry standard printing file, save yourself money and design your own literature. If you need help, hire a designer who has a few years of experience in the printing industry and a good sense of design.

There are a lot of things you can do to help increase sales, many of which creative design plays an integral part. Brochures, newsletters, trade show booths, vehicle wraps, and web sites all incorporate some type of design.

Even social media utilizes design. Do you really want to use the same template background on Twitter that thousands of others are using? No! Get a custom background created for your business. Are you part of a franchise or multi-level marketing (MLM) company such as Mary Kay® or Scentsy®?

If so, use design to make your business unique and different from the million other sales consultants.

> **TIP:** Do your homework when hiring a designer. How long has the designer been in business? When you look at the designer's portfolio, does their style appeal to you? Does the designer respond to you in a timely manner? Do they provide a contract outlining deliverables and includes time lines? Be sure you have chosen a designer who is right for you. Ask these questions before you begin working on a project.

Brainstorm the kind of marketing campaigns you would like to implement. Gather examples and ideas to help build direction and the look and feel for your next campaign. Find your design style, stick to it, and use it consistently. Through a professional business image you will win customers!

34 THINGS ENTREPRENEURS SHOULD DO DAILY

1. Complete Daily Forward Focus Log FIRST.

2. 10 tweets or retweets — remember the 80/20 rule: 80% of tweets should be about others — not YOU.

3. 2 to 5 Facebook Page updates.

4. Attend networking meeting or add one to calendar for future date.

5. Be flexible and allow for changes in the day — we must be ready to adapt.

6. Call for help when you begin to feel overwhelmed... not when you are so entrenched you can't see how to "come up for air."

7. Check in with entrepreneurial Facebook Group to interact with other business owners and catch up on news.

8. Comment on a professional blog belonging to another company.

9. Confirm tomorrow's appointments.

10. Devote 45 minutes with no interruptions to reading business or entrepreneur books or periodicals.

11. Do one small thing every day that is different from your normal routine — this helps avoid falling into a rut or losing steam.

12. Dress appropriately. Get dressed and do everything you would on a day that you have a client appointment or networking engagement — even when your calendar is empty!

13. Focus 30 minutes strictly on marketing.

14. Follow up with clients — both perspective and existing clients.

15. Make deposits as necessary.

16. Pick one Forward Focus item that will make the most drastic difference in your business or you clients... focus your attention there!

17. Remind yourself that it is OK to say No.

18. Remove office clutter — continuing to be organized is crucial to success.

19. Respond to email. Read all email before responding to any to be sure you are replying with the most up to date information.

20. Return ALL phone calls.

21. Review any appointments and scheduled tasks.

22. Review calendar for this week and next, as well as month at a glance.

23. Review tomorrow's schedule at the end of the day.

24. Review website analytics.

25. Review website for possible changes and errors.

26. Search meet-up.com for appropriate networking or speaking opportunities.

27. Send a thank you card to a strategic partner, referral partner, previous client, local connector, etc.

28. Set specific time frames for focus throughout the day.

29. Shut down and close up at a reasonable time. Working from home makes it very easy to lose track of time.

30. Spend 15 minutes seriously asking this question: What would I do with my business if time and money were no object?

31. Stay current with Google Alerts and respond as needed.

32. Take a brisk 10 minute walk or do 5 minutes of muscle stretches. Believe it or not, this is a well-kept secret of successful entrepreneurs!

33. Visit with or call a local connector, accountability partner, mastermind participant, etc. It is too easy to get "stuck" at the computer. Make sure to reach out at least once every day!

34. Work on any mastermind or accountability partner tasks or assignments.

HOW TO BECOME AN
E3 CO-AUTHOR

E3 is always looking for experts to share their knowledge. Authors are asked to write a chapter that will specifically help entrepreneurs learn the ins and outs of creating and operating a successful business. The E3 book series will feature no more than six authors per book, thus allowing you a generous amount of space to share your industry tips and business success story. We are not interested in limiting your word count like other collaborative book publishers. We believe "the more, the better." Your readers will have the opportunity to really get to know you and what you do.

And there is an added plus to being a published author: it gives you credibility and recognition. You will be looked at as THE EXPERT in your field. The E3 team also wants to help you grow your endeavors this is why we partner you with up to five other experts to co-author an E3 book. Not only will we be promoting your book, but so will five other people! You have instant networking!

If you wish to be a part of the E3 book series, please contact us though our website etimes3.info/contact-us and include the following information:

- Name
- Email
- Phone
- Company
- Expertise
- Topics: list up to three topics that you REALLY want to write about in which you have a lot of experience.
- References: list three people we can call or email to ask about you. Yes, we will ask them if they think you are an expert on the topics you listed.

For more information, please visit etimes3.info.